LET'S VISIT GUYANA

Let's visit
GUYANA

ANDY GRAVETTE

ACKNOWLEDGEMENTS

The Author and Publishers are grateful to the following organizations and individuals for permission to reproduce copyright illustrations in this book:

Carolyn Bennett of Bookers Sugar Company Limited; J. Allan Cash Limited; Commonwealth Development Corporation; COMPIX, Commonwealth Institute; Bill Derbyshire; Hutchison Photo Library; G. W. Lennox; Scotch Film; Taylor Woodrow International Limited; World Bank; World Development Education.

First published 1988

Published by
MACMILLAN PUBLISHERS LTD
Houndmills, Basingstoke, Hampshire RG21 2XS
and London
Companies and representatives
throughout the world

Designed and produced by Burke Publishing Company Limited
Pegasus House, 116-120 Golden Lane
London EC1Y 0TL, England.

Printed in Hong Kong

British Library Cataloguing in Publication Data
Gravette, A. Gerald (Andrew Gerald)
    Let's visit Guyana.
    1. Guyana
    I. Title
    988'.103
    ISBN 0-333-48504-1

Contents

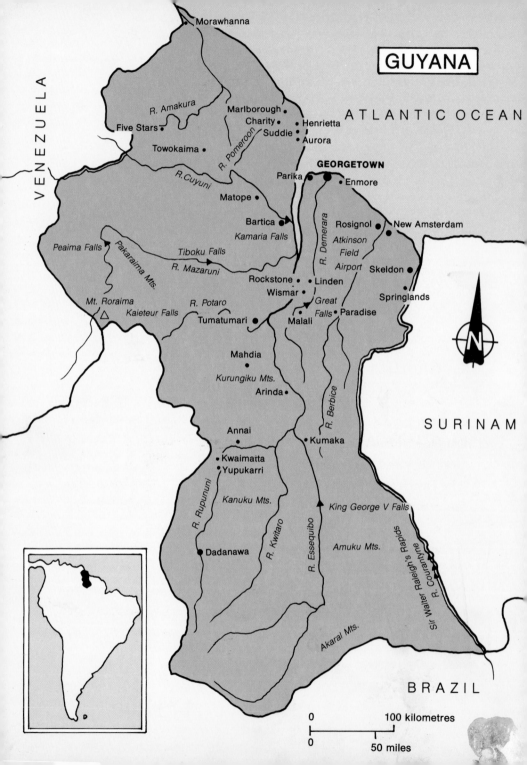

Land of Many Waters

The earliest inhabitants of Guyana were the Amerindians. They gave the country the name "Land of Many Waters". It is still a land dominated by rivers but now Guyana is a mixture of contrasting scenery, a varied climate and a nation comprised of many races.

Located on the "bulge" of the great South American continent, Guyana is hot and tropical with mountains, dense jungle and a flat coastal region. The heat makes it a difficult country to live in, particularly for people from a temperate climate. In addition, the nation's poor economy has placed it in the shadow of its neighbours such as oil-rich Venezuela and the vast country of Brazil.

Today, Guyana is known for several different reasons. A cook would know the famous Demerara sugar; shoppers for wines or spirits may be familiar with Guyana's rum; and the postage-stamp collector will know that the world's rarest stamp is the One Cent British Guiana—the original name for this former British

**A nineteenth-century
engraving of an
Amerindian wading in a
river**

colony. But few people elsewhere in the world know very much about this unusual country of contrasts.

Looking at the tapering shape of South America on a map of the world, and following the chain of Caribbean islands down to where they seem to meet the continent's coast, leads the eye to Guyana. The country is about the size of England and Scotland together—215,000 square kilometres (83,000 square miles).

Guyana's coastline faces the Atlantic Ocean. To the west lies Venezuela; to the south and west is the north of Brazil (South America's largest country); and to the east of Guyana is Surinam.

8

At the coast there are several large river estuaries. Three main rivers give their names to the country's counties or divisions. Essequibo, Demerara and Berbice divide the land politically but Guyana also has four major physical regions. The low coastal plains—a narrow strip of land along the coast where ninety per cent of the population live and work; the hilly, sand and clay belt further inland; the highland region where peaks reach over 2,800 metres (9,200 feet) in height, and the inland savannah region known as the Rupununi. This is also a grassy plateau at a

Demerara sugar being poured into a ship's hold. Sugar is one of Guyana's major exports

height of about 500 metres (1,640 feet); it marks the watershed with the giant Amazon River basin.

Almost seventy-five per cent of Guyana is covered in equatorial rainforest which is largely unexplored and is a source of valuable timber and minerals. It is in this region and on the Kanuku slopes that the true Guyanese people can be found. Few Amerindians now remain in this part of South America although their history goes back many thousands of years. These indigenous Indians now eke out a living by cultivating root crops and raising pigs and a few chickens on homesteads in the interior of the country.

Guyana's original inhabitants formed three groups known by their languages as Arawak, Warrau and Carib. The Arawaks were the first settlers in the Caribbean islands—the region got its

Fishermen with their catch. Black Guyanese, like these men, form one of the main ethnic groups within the population today

name from the cannibalistic Caribs who followed the Arawaks throughout the West Indies. Those Indians who remained in this part of the continent either hunted in the forests, or grew crops such as cassava root, maize, yam and tropical fruits. They were the inventors of the hammock and the canoe. They smoked tobacco and grew potatoes long before European people discovered them. These Amerindians now represent only about four per cent of the population of the country.

In parts of today's Guyana visitors would be forgiven for thinking they were in Madras or Calcutta in India. In areas of the coastal plain almost the entire population has its roots in the Indian subcontinent. In other regions most of the people are black or Afro-Guyanese, while in some mining communities the predominant races are European and Chinese. It is Guyana's historical background which has resulted in this country being a "melting-pot" of races from all over the world. The population of the country now stands at around one million, compared with those of England and Scotland which total around fifty-three million people in an area roughly similar in size to Guyana.

Called the "Land of Six Peoples", Guyana really has only two major racial divisions, the black Guyanese and the Asian Indian community. The Indians now represent at least half of the total population. Many of these immigrants use their own languages such as Hindustani, Hindi and Urdu. In some communities Chinese or Portuguese is spoken, but the official language of Guyana is English. It is the only English-speaking country in South America although a Creole dialect (a mixture of

11

A view of one of Guyana's swampy coastal plains. It is these coastal areas which are the most thickly populated

languages used by descendants of European settlers) is spoken in some rural areas. The largest religious group is Christian, the second is Hindu and Muslims comprise about ten per cent of the population.

The countryside of Guyana varies from flat, swampy lowlands along the coast to high, forested mountain peaks and, with all this contrast, the climate is quite spectacular. The coastal zone benefits from the sea breeze which cools the constant temperature of between 26 and 28 degrees Celsius (79 and 82 degrees Fahrenheit). The nights are also quite cool. And the humidity in this part of Guyana is rather high as is the rainfall. The rainy seasons last from May to August and from November to January. Inland, especially in the highlands, fluctuations in temperature are more pronounced. In the south, temperatures can get extremely high, particularly in the dry season from August to May. The hottest weather takes the thermometer up to 39 degrees Celsius (103 degrees Fahrenheit), while temperatures in the mountains can drop to as low as 11 degrees Celsius (20 degrees Fahrenheit). Rainfall in this region varies with altitude and rarely exceeds 1,500 millimetres (60 inches) during the single wet season from April to September. No earthquakes, tornadoes or hurricanes beleaguer Guyana, which is outside the belt of Caribbean storms.

All this rainfall precipitated on the highlands, savannah and coastal plains means that the land requires adequate drainage in the form of rivers. The largest of these is the Essequibo River

A stretch of the Potaro River, one of the four tributaries of the longest river in Guyana—the mighty Essequibo

which is 9,500 kilometres (600 miles) long and drains about fifty per cent of Guyana. This river is navigable for less than one tenth of its length and has four tributaries. On one of these rivers, the Potaro, the Kaiteur Falls drop nearly five times the height of the Niagara Falls—226 metres (741 feet).

The Courantyne River which separates Guyana from Surinam can take shipping on 95 kilometres (60 miles) of its length; the Berbice River, between the Essequibo and the Courantyne, is navigable for 160 kilometres (100 miles). The other major river is the Demerara. It is this waterway which is

A worker spraying stagnant water with insecticide—an operation which is intended to destroy the malaria-spreading mosquito larvae

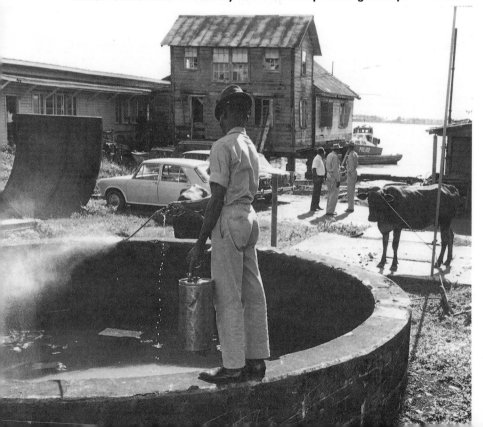

used for the transporting of mineral products to the coast from the interior.

The climate of Guyana is not the ideal environment in which to live and work but the people have adapted well to the humidity and heat as most of them originated in the tropical lands of either India or Africa. The population is now generally healthy although malaria (contracted from the bite of mosquitoes) and diseases like yellow fever have not been totally eradicated. The Guyanese are well fed because of the fertile soil on the coastal plain, although their diet is uninteresting and consists mainly of rice with some fish or meat.

The traveller to Guyana will particularly notice the friendly and hospitable nature of the Guyanese people. They are especially fond of inviting foreigners to their homes.

Discovery and Early Settlers

It is generally thought that Christopher Columbus, the Genoese explorer, first sighted the coastline of what is now Guyana in 1498, early in his third voyage to the Americas. Certainly Amerigo Vespucci, together with Alonso de Ojeda (a mapmaker who had joined Columbus' first voyage) both sailed along the entire north-eastern shoulder of South America in 1499. The coast was charted at that time from Surinam to the Gulf of Venezuela. This region includes the 430-kilometre (267-mile) Atlantic coast of Guyana.

Another Spanish navigator named Vicente Pinzon, once captain of Columbus' ship, the *Nina,* visited the coast in 1500 and again in 1508. At this time the continent of South America was unexplored by Europeans and was known as *Novo Mondo*— Spanish for the "New World." Guiana was the name given to the lands between the Amazon and the Orinoco river estuaries. Probably the earliest known map of Guyana was that drawn by Juan de la Cosa in 1500.

Later, there was a great deal of interest in the new discoveries of the Americas. The main attraction was treasure in the form of gold, silver and gems. Spanish *conquistadores* (conquerors) opened up the lands of Central America—Mexico, Yucatan and Panama. Great treasures were found in these countries and in some of the islands in the Caribbean. The Portuguese were also searching for riches. They too concentrated their explorations in South America at this time.

Although both the Spanish and Portuguese powers knew of the existence of the lands along the north-east coast of South America, neither was interested in making anything but half-hearted exploratory visits which produced no evidence of gold. For over one hundred years after its first sighting by Columbus, Guyana remained the undisturbed territory of the Arawak, Warrau and Carib Indian tribes. Muddy harbours and sandbanks along the coast prevented any good mooring sites being established and the land was almost forgotten until the French, English and Dutch began to acquire territories in the nearby Caribbean.

Sir Walter Raleigh, perhaps one of the most famous adventurers of the time, landed on the Guyanese coast in 1595. He thought that the rivers here held the secret to *El Dorado*—the fabled City of Gold. Today, 640 kilometres (four hundred miles) up the Courantyne River, there is a natural phenomenon named in memory of the great sailor's exploits in the Guianas—Sir Walter Raleigh's Rapids. Needless to say, Raleigh's efforts proved fruitless and he abandoned his search.

17

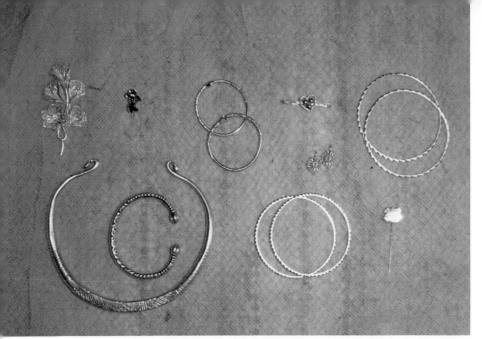

Ornate gold and silver jewellery made in the traditional Guyanese fashion. It was these precious metals which first attracted the European sixteenth-century adventurers to *El Dorado*

It was not until 1616 that the Dutch first established a foothold in Guyana. They founded the settlement of Kijkorveral and, by 1621, the tiny colony was placed under the protection of the West India Company of the Netherlands.

Another settlement was established in 1624; and a third, at Demerara, in 1645. These three colonies (one on each of the Essequibo, Berbice and Demerara Rivers) were administered by the West India Company for 170 years, until 1791. Many British subjects migrated to these first European communities in the Guianas—as they were then known.

The Dutch had begun cultivating sugar-cane on Guyana's flat,

18

fertile, coastal strip. Their success attracted other entrepreneurs from Europe. As early as the year 1700 sugar was an established crop and planters flooded into the new territory. By this time, the three lands which eventually became Surinam, French Guiana and the present-day Guyana, had begun to take shape as separate entities.

French traders had settled in French Guiana (Guyane) in 1626, while the Dutch had accepted the territory of Surinam from the English in 1667, in exchange for North American colonies including New York. Guyana, the section of the Guianas furthest to the west, proved to be the most fertile and, by the early eighteenth century, was a major producer of sugar-cane. The Dutch had found that Amerindians did not make good plantation-workers and, in order to maintain the considerable work force necessary for large-scale sugar cultivation, they imported slaves from Africa. By 1760, the British living in the settlement of Demerara outnumbered the Dutch colonists.

In 1781 the British overran the three Dutch townships and claimed the country as their own. Georgetown, now the capital city, was then founded. This was a short-lived victory, however, as the French captured the colony in the following year. This was also a brief triumph as, in 1794, the Dutch regained their hold on the South American territory and they retained their supremacy in Guyana for just two years. The British again established themselves as colonizers, and again their reign was thwarted; this time by the Dutch, in 1802. After one year of Dutch rule the

19

A view of the territories in Guyana which were under the control of the British at the end of the nineteenth century

British again gained control. In the twenty-three years from 1780 to 1803 the country which is now Guyana changed hands six times!

For almost two hundred years following the first occupation of the country in 1621, the sugar industry flourished. Guyanan planters were wealthy in terms of the early exploitation of European colonies in the West Indies. The British, who had finally taken over administration of the country in 1803, had no

20

desire to lose such a precious asset for a third time. In 1814, they negotiated a deal with the Dutch settlers whereby the entire country was ceded to the British Crown "in perpetuity". Even by this time the area of coast and narrow plain, backed by impenetrable jungle and fed by large rivers, had no established name. It was not until 1831 that the British formally decided that their outpost in South America should be given the name of British Guiana.

The Dutch and the British

A feudal system was established in Guyana from the earliest days of the Dutch West India Company. It was called the *patroon* system and gave merchants or landowners who settled in the country a status similar to that of Lord of the Manor. Most of these early settlers on the Guyana coast based themselves at the fort of Kijkroveral. They purchased areas of land and imported settlers and field-workers for their sugar and tobacco plantations.

The Dutch found that the best place for sugar cultivation was the edge of the inland plain and in the White Sands zone. The skills of reclaiming land from rivers or from the sea, which the Dutch had learned in their homeland of Holland, were used to dry out areas for planting vegetables and fruit-trees. Owners of large areas of land, or plantations, were called "planters". In the middle of the seventeenth century, the landowners realized that they would need more labourers to work in the plantations. Many thousands of black slaves were brought from West and

Guyanese today—the ancestors of these people were brought to Guyana from Africa as slaves to work on the sugar plantations under conditions of very severe hardship and deprivation

Central Africa in cruel conditions, sailing from the "Dark Continent" to the "New World". Many slaves died, either on the journey or when they arrived in Guyana. But the landowners found that, because of their dark skin (which is more resistant to the heat of the sun's rays than a white skin), the black workers adapted better to the familiar tropical climate. With extra labour and a regular supply of slaves, the Dutch planters flourished and large areas of land were soon cleared and planted with valuable crops.

23

Elegant wooden buildings of the colonial period. They bear witness to the wealth and lifestyle of the plantation-owners from Europe

For almost 150 years after the first European settlement was founded on Guyana, sugar and tobacco plantations expanded and the landowners prospered. It was in 1763 that the black slave population staged an uprising—the Cuffy Rebellion. Cuffy, a black slave who headed a revolt against the cruelty of the plantation masters, was slaughtered and his followers were atrociously punished. Cuffy is now a national hero and, in Brickdam (one of the main thoroughfares of Georgetown, the modern capital) a spectacular statue of the slave leader stands on a stepped plinth.

The unsettled period after the rebellion divided the community in Guyana even more than the differences of race, religion and wealth. British settlers in parts of the country outnumbered the Dutch colonists, yet they were constantly reminded of their position as visiting merchants and landowners in a Dutch state. By 1781, the situation between the rival nationalities had become so tense that the British rose up against the Dutch and captured the major towns. This was the beginning of a "see-saw" effect—of governments changing every few years for the next twenty-one years.

During this time the Dutch West Indies Company was disbanded (1791); the American War of Independence (1775-76) was fought; and the French Revolution (1789) preoccupied the French in their own section of the Guianas—now Guyane—and in their island colonies in the Caribbean. Despite all these changes, the slave population continued to multiply and to labour in the fields.

The turmoil in the newly-established countries of the West Indies and South America gradually quietened down. By the end of the eighteenth century, the Spanish, French, Dutch and British divided the islands and territories between themselves. Treaty after treaty defined boundaries and legal areas of administration and, by 1814, after much haggling, the British were finally established as the governors of Guyana and the country became a colony of the British Crown.

After Britain took over Guyana initially, in 1803, many changes occurred in the administrative and social structure of the colony. In 1831, as the region of the Guianas had no recognized name, the British drew up a map of the territory and named it British Guiana. In 1834 the British abolished slavery officially throughout their colonies worldwide. However, emancipation—freedom—did not come to the slaves in British Guiana until the year 1837, the first year of the reign of Queen Victoria.

After about five years, planters became concerned about the harvesting of their huge crops. Much sugar and tobacco was wasted because the labour was unreliable, there were no slaves to work all hours of the day and few wanted to do the harder jobs on the plantations. Sugar-cane mills came to a standstill, fields of cane were burned and ruined, and tobacco rotted on the plants. By 1844, the British had to resort to searching for cheap labour from anywhere in the world.

The British looked east, to their colonies in Asia, for new sources of workers. In India they found many thousands of people who had bad conditions in their own country, and who wanted to work in the West Indies and in South America. Many Portuguese, who had been turned out of neighbouring Brazil, had already taken up residence in Guyana as plantation-workers in the 1840s. The British were also being asked if they would take on Chinese and East Indian workers to run the sugar-mills and rum factories. All these new labourers wanted to be paid for their work and so they were made to sign a document called an "indenture". This was an agreement in which the workers said they would work in the fields or in the factories for a small amount of money, plus clothes, food and accommodation, for a minimum of about five years. After that, they could leave their employment or renegotiate their work contract. In this way, for the next seventy-three years, until 1914, British plantation-owners kept their crop production up and maintained the economy of the country.

Sugar and Slaves

Unlike tobacco, which needs a special climate, constant attention and careful nurturing, sugar-cane is an easy crop to grow almost anywhere in the tropics. The cane, which is a type of grass that originated in Asia, possibly near India, was introduced into the New World by Christopher Columbus. Columbus found that sugar-cane grew very well in such places as Cuba, Hispaniola and Jamaica.

Within a few years, sugar-cane was being grown commercially throughout the West Indies. By the eighteenth century most of the twenty main islands of the Caribbean were dependent on cane for their economic survival. The British Leeward Islands were even known as "The Sugar Isles".

Each island had to import large numbers of slaves to plant, tend, harvest and process the cane. As sugar became popular in Europe, almost every country in the region exported large quantities of processed sugar across the Atlantic and, later, to the new American states.

28

Workers digging an irrigation ditch in a sugar plantation. Sugar grows easily and well in tropical conditions

Parts of the Guianas were not to be left out of the rich growth industry that sugar had become. By the latter half of the seventeenth century, sugar was an important export from the regions which are now known as Surinam and Guyana. Today, the sugar industry in Surinam has declined. But, in Guyana, sugar is the main export crop.

Mature sugar-cane looks something like a piece of thick bamboo, or a stick with bright green, long, feathery leaves. At regular intervals there appears a "knee" or joint on the hollow stem which is full of a pithy fibre. To plant sugar-cane a short section, including a "knee", is cut from the three-metre (nine foot) long mature cane. This is known as a "ratoon" and it is planted in the ground with a little fertilizer. Fifteen to twenty months later, the sugar-cane has reached its full height and is ready for harvesting. From then on, the plant can be harvested at intervals for something over fifteen years. Sugar-cane fields cover very large areas of the countryside and are planted out in orderly rows.

In the seventeenth and eighteenth centuries, as still happens today in some cases, great fields of sugar-cane were planted by hand and harvested by hand. The cane-cutter uses a long, wide-bladed knife, known as a "machete". With one clean cut, the long stalk is severed just above the ground and, before it falls, the

A sugar plantation being "burnt off"

A harvesting machine which cuts and slices the cane stalks—work otherwise done by hand using a machete, as in the early days

cane-cutter trims off the leaves and the wavy frond at the top of the stem. This is a tough, hot and tiring job under scorching sun and in dry conditions. Sometimes the sugar-cane fields are "burnt off". The cane itself only chars and does not burn completely in this process which concentrates the pithy, sugar-laden core of the cane, but makes the work dirty and the air thick with black soot and burnt leaves.

Cane-cutting was not the type of work that plantation owners would do themselves. Instead, they imported slaves from Africa by the thousands, to provide a cheap work force to cut cane for

A 1930s photograph of a barge loaded with cut sugar-cane, hauled by a single horse. Today, transport is usually mechanized

them. The African's dark skin was used to the hot, tropical sun, and the slaves were generally fit and strong enough to spend long hours cutting cane in the fields. So, in Guyana, as in the rest of the West Indies, the planters, or plantation owners, employed large "armies" of slaves to do the hard work. Slaves were given basic food, clothing and shelter but very little else in return for their labour.

Once cut, the cane was sliced by machete into lengths about as long as a man's forearm and piled into ox-carts. Cane-workers would spend all day out in the fields cutting and loading the

32

brown-green stalks. In the central factory, the sugar was extracted from the cane stalks. First, the stalks were crushed by giant mills to release from the pith a thick, syrup-like liquid which was partly sugar. The mills which crushed the sugar-cane were powered by wind, water, oxen, horses or even men. Few primitive mills are now in operation. Most processing is done today in giant factories powered by huge furnaces, by steam and by electricity.

The liquid which came from crushing sugar-cane stalks, was a greenish colour and was called *guarapo*—juice. The squashed fibre, cane shucks and bits of leaves left after the crushing process, was called *bagasse* and it was often discarded or burned. Nowadays, *bagasse* is used in making chipboard, paper, cardboard and packing material. The *guarapo* was boiled over large fires and lime juice was added to it to make a golden brown syrup. When the mixture cooled, a dark liquid which sank to the bottom of the big boiling vats was separated from a clear liquid which floated to the top. The dark syrup was called molasses. It is from the molasses that we now get treacle, syrup, some chemicals and alcohol. The alcohol obtained from molasses is used in hospitals and also in the production of rum—forming an important export commodity. Today, this by-product of sugar-cane is an essential ingredient in many scientific, industrial and domestic processes.

Over fires which were more carefully controlled than those used to separate it from the molasses, the clear liquid was again boiled until a chemical change took place. As if by magic, when the clear liquid reached a certain heat, it transformed into a mass of yellowish crystals—sugar. Nowadays, the process is very similar to that of the old days, but it is on a much larger scale. It is cleaner, controlled by computers, and all done mechanically. Now, the sugar crystals are also purified to produce castor, icing and granulated sugar. Many more scientifically useful by-products are extracted from what is originally just a large grass stalk!

In Guyana, as in many of the Caribbean countries, almost every slave, apart from some convicted criminals, was brought from Africa. They came from many different parts of the continent and from different races and tribes. Few spoke the same language; some were very tall and some were pigmies. The country was new to them, as were the white-skinned masters with their curious clothes and habits. Gone were their days of hunting in the African bush, lazily fishing the great rivers of Senegal and Nigeria and celebrating with feasts and tribal dances. Suddenly, without warning, they had been chained to each other, transported across the ocean and then forced to use a machete to cut cane every day. Most plantation masters were strict but they realized that the slaves had their own way of life which was different from that of their masters.

The African slaves maintained their own culture and traditions in Guyana, even though they were working on the plantations. They built houses similar to the palm-roofed huts they had left behind; and they cultivated some of the African

Modern smallholders with their donkeys. Many small farms in Guyana date back to the period of emancipation when the freed slaves brought plots of land with their first savings

food plants which they had brought across the ocean. They continued their dancing and their music, and lived in much the same way as they had in Africa.

The difference was that they were enslaved. Thinking they were being kind to them, the planters often built large barracks, or barracoons, of brick and stone—more like cells—in which they made the reluctant slaves live. Gradually, the white masters made the Africans forget their homelands and their background. They taught the slaves their own languages—first Dutch, then English. They educated them in European religions, in dressing and in the way of life of white settlers in the Caribbean.

Finally, after more than two hundred years of slavery,

emancipation (freedom) came to the descendants of those early African victims of the slave-traders. The British government told the planters and settlers to free all the slaves who were working for them. The British law of 1834 required that all servants and slaves must be freed, or offered their freedom. It was, however, another three years before the abolition of slavery was put into practice in Guyana.

Under the slavery system on the sugar-cane and tobacco plantations, slaves were fed, clothed and given shelter in huts or in barracoons. They worked long hours in the fields, in a sugar-extraction mills, or in the rum-making factories. But they did not have to worry about where their food, water, clothes, housing and medical attention came from—it was up to the plantation-owner to keep his slaves fit and healthy to work hard for him. When all this was taken away from the slave, he had no home, no food, and he could no longer call on the overseer's doctor if he or his children got ill.

As a result, many slaves continued to work on the plantations after emancipation—only then they worked for payment. Some left the plantations to live by the sea, or moved up the rivers to find their own plot of land. Some slaves saved the pittance they earned in the plantation after slavery to buy their own little smallholding.

Most slaves tried out their new-found freedom only to return to work for a wage in the master's plantations. Often, by the time they had found that life was very difficult in nineteenth-century Guyana, the planters had replaced them with indentured workers from the East Indies, or from India. However, as the country increased in wealth and towns expanded, roads were built and workers were needed in the urban areas. Then freed slaves found employment building the highways and railroads, working with shipping and opening their own small businesses. Many freed slaves left Guyana to work on projects in other countries, such as the Panama Railway 1848-55, construction work in nearby South American countries and work on some of the Caribbean islands.

In order to find work and also to follow relatives who emigrated after the Second World War, a number of Guyanese people are still migrating each year.

Three Regions—Six Peoples

In early times "The Guianas" of South America stretched roughly from the Orinoco River mouth, almost as far east as the Amazon delta. Inland, the boundaries of this part of the continent were the Sierras (mountains) of Acarai and the Sierra de Tumucumaque. In area, The Guianas covered almost 400,000 square kilometres (nearly 200,000 square miles)—about the size of all the Japanese islands put together.

Before exploration and division by Europeans, the region was known to outsiders generally as Terra Incognita ("Unknown Lands"), Terra Nova ("New Lands"), or just Paria (the Indian name for the bay). The local Indian population called it Guyana—"Land of Many Waters". With the search for *El Dorado*—the fabled City of Gold, thought to be somewhere in the highlands behind the Guiana coastline—several excursions were made into the hinterland during the seventeenth century. Most of the region was, and still remains, impenetrable jungle with access possible only by way of the wide, fast-flowing rivers. In the early days, disease, the inhospitable climate and regular attacks by ferocious Amerindians, discouraged even the most determined explorers who ventured further than the coastal plains or riverside settlements.

A large slice of land, right in the centre of The Guianas, was exchanged in 1667 by the British for a Dutch colony in North America—New Amsterdam, which became New York. The piece of The Guianas acquired by the Dutch became known as Surinam, or Dutch Guiana. The most easterly sector of the Guianas was occupied by the French and the westernmost section remained British territory. This, therefore, resulted in the rough division of The Guianas into three, similarly-sized areas—British Guiana, Dutch Guiana and French Guiana.

It was not until 1851 that the British settlers decided to define the borders of their territory on a map. They chose the Courantyne River as the country's eastern border (with Surinam, or Suriname). To the south was the border with the vast country of Brazil. To the west, the border with Venezuela was, and still is, in constant dispute. However, the British managed to establish a commonly accepted border for purposes of mapping and charts, and they named the country British Guiana after the Indian name for the area. Thus, for the first time, the country became officially known as Guyana.

With the other two divisions of The Guianas taking their own courses and developing their own resources, Guyana set about dividing the country into administrative regions. The largest district, known as Rupununi, encompassed the high mountain

39

area in the south of the country. The second largest administrative region was the Mazaruni-Potaro, a district containing the giant Pakaraima mountain range. North of this were the coastal districts starting with Georgetown, the capital in the East Demerara district; Fort Wellington, in the West Berbice district; and New Amsterdam in the East Berbice district. To the west of the capital were the districts of West Demerara (including Atkinson Field, near the Timehri International Airport, and the township of Paprika), and Essequibo, where the towns of Charity and Marlborough are located. Today, some of the old administrative districts have merged and Guyana is divided into six administrative regions and five municipalities, plus several small, outlying villages and communities.

As the district of East Demerara is home of the capital city, it houses the largest population of any district—well over a quarter of a million people. The most sparsely populated district is the large region to the south, the Rupununi District.

It is interesting to note the names of some towns in these administrative districts. There are a number of English-sounding place names such as Georgetown, the capital, and Atkinson Field. There are Scottish-sounding names such as MacKenzie; some descriptive place names such as Rockstone, Charity and Five Stars; some French-sounding names, and some Dutch names such as Vreed-en-Hoop. By far the majority of place names are, however, taken from Amerindian words, roughly translated. The rivers, for example, mostly have Indian names—Mazaruni, Potaro, Essequibo and Demerara.

Fishing in the Demarara River. Most Guyanese rivers bear local traditional names first given to them by the Amerindians

The origins of these names in Guyana go back in history to the early European pioneers who "opened up" the country. In most cases, the explorers of old would rely on the local population to tell them what they called a river, mountain, forest clearing, hill or waterfall. Sometimes there would be an Indian settlement at a particular spot by a river or hill. If the explorers wanted to settle and build their own houses by the Indian huts, they would often call the entire settlement by the Indian name—Kumaka, Arinda or Malai, for example. Sometimes the settlers would establish a village or town and name it after some event which happened there. Tiger Falls, for example, was possibly the spot where the explorers saw a black jaguar—the local version of a puma.

The language used in early Guyana was also a reflection of the

A modern reconstruction of an Amerindian meeting-house, called
Umana Yana. Modern Guyanese are proud of their traditional roots

people who came to live in the country. Because, for almost two
hundred years, the country changed hands between the British
and the Dutch, many Dutch words continued to be used in the
patois (dialect, or local language) of early Guyana. African
slaves, from many different west coast races and tribes, brought
some of their own African words with them. These words were
also assimilated into the language of Guyana, producing what is
known as a Creole, or mixed, speech which includes European
and African words mingled together. After the emancipation of
slaves a new influx of foreign races arrived in the country and
they too put some of their words into the "melting pot"
vocabulary. These were the immigrants from the Indian
subcontinent, from the Portuguese dependencies in the Atlantic

42

Ocean, from the East Indies and from China. Indians brought a number of dialects and regional languages to Guyana, as did the East Indian migrants, the Portuguese settlers and those who came from Chinese-speaking countries such as Singapore and Hong Kong.

By the mid-nineteenth century, at least five distinctly different races and nationalities had settled in the towns and villages of Guyana. These settlers spoke languages as different from the local Arawak, Warrau and Carib, as any European language is from Chinese, or Hindi is from Congolese. However, it was in Guyana that these languages evolved to establish a "mother tongue" and an official language. Generally, a country with its own indigenous population has an established official language. In Guyana, however, because of their primitive lifestyles, the Amerindians, whose original home it was, were overshadowed by the more sophisticated Europeans. The Europeans who gained control eventually—the British—imposed their own language and way of life on the country and people of Guyana. This process, called colonialism, occurred throughout the undeveloped world during the seventeenth, eighteenth and nineteenth centuries. English became the official language of Guyana and the Amerindian languages were relegated to the provinces. In the Creole (or mixed) language of the country, several Amerindian words survive, as also do many Dutch words. African words have also crept into the Creole language through music and dance. Many East Indian words and expressions from the subcontinent of India have also been assimilated into the everyday language of Guyana. Hindi and Urdu are now spoken in some parts of Guyana.

The Indian celebration of Hindu and Muslim holidays such as Phagwah, Deepavali and Eid-ul-Azha have become part of the Guyanese way of life. This is evidence of the fact that, in addition to the overriding influence of the British, inside little more than a century, other nation's languages, religions and behaviour have imposed themselves on the pattern of everyday life. Instead of the original pagan religions of the Amerindian tribes, the predominant religions of Guyana are now Christianity, Hinduism and Islam. The overall population figures place the East Indians as the highest percentage at about fifty per cent. Figures show that the African, or African-derived population stands at about forty-three per cent of the population and the rest—the remaining seven per cent—is comprised of Europeans, Chinese and Amerindians.

Visitors to Guyana are struck by the way Guyanese people work. Some eighty people out of every hundred of the population are actually in employment. It is said that ninety per cent of the working population of Guyana work on the coastal strip of cultivatable land between the sea and the sandy, clay hills. As with most developing countries, food production is a priority and agricultural development takes first place in the economy of Guyana. Rice is an important crop in Guyana and many people's lives are centred on the production of this staple diet. Whether working in the fields or minding a shop, tending a stall in the

A large cattle farm in Guyana. As in other developing dountries, the government encourages food production as a priority

local market-place or tilling a village plot of land, the Guyanese are a busy nation who always seem to be active—whether or not they are very productive!

In tropical Guyana, because of the climate, people spend much of their time in the open air instead of in houses and offices. In the towns of Guyana many houses are made of wood, and verandas and shutters help to keep the occupants cool. (Georgetown is considered to be the best-preserved wooden city anywhere in the Caribbean.) Because of the mosquitoes, mosquito netting often covers the windows and some people sleep under mosquito nets. Newer housing developments are being constructed of prefabricated blocks and concrete.

45

A wooden house on stilts. Having the building elevated above the ground keeps the inside cool even during the hottest months

Visiting a typical family is the best way to get to know how the Guyanese people live. Take an imaginary family, call them the Greens (a not uncommon name in Guyana). Mr Green may work with the Guyana Fisheries Company in Georgetown as an accountant, working a thirty-eight-hour week. Mr Green may have graduated from the University of Guyana. (Guyana is the only English-speaking country in the Caribbean with its own national university.) Part of the Greens' house, with its tin roof and bright green shutters may be raised on stilts. This keeps the inside of the white-painted, wooden structure cool. Mr Green probably walks to his place of work near the harbour or possibly he may have a bicycle. Mrs Green may not work, but she may earn some "pin money" by creating artistic weaving or beadwork

46

which is sold as souvenirs in the Guyana Crafts Cooperative just along the Main Street.

The Greens may have three children; Yvonne, just ten years old, is attending her last year at primary school. Education is free and compulsory in Guyana for children between the ages of five and fourteen. Probably, before going to primary school, Yvonne attended the local nursery school. Guyana has one of the highest literacy rates in the world—more than ninety per cent. Edith, Yvonne's elder sister aged 17, will probably have just started her first term at one of the two schools in the country for home economics and domestic crafts. Edith will have completed six years at primary school and a further five years at lower secondary school. If it is Easter Monday, neither Yvonne or

Guyanese schoolchildren

Workers inspecting coffee beans on a plantation. Many Guyanese study agriculture before going to work on a farm or plantation

Edith will be at school, they will probably be flying traditional kites with young people—on one of the long, green boulevards down by the canal or along the sea wall where Atlantic breezes catch the colourful shapes of the holiday kites. If either sister should fall over, or hurt herself, or if they are taken ill, they could be taken to one of the free clinics or to the General Hospital in the city.

Andrew, the family's eldest son, may be interested in farming and may specialize in agricultural studies. There are three

48

farming colleges that he might attend: the Guyana School of Agriculture, the Mon-Repos Agricultural College and the Burnham Agricultural Institute. The Kuru-Kuru Cooperative Training College also gives an introduction to farming methods and land use; this is because agriculture is the most important occupation in Guyana.

Although National Service was introduced in 1974, Andrew may not qualify for this because of his academic studies. If it is Easter, Andrew may be at home with the family for the holiday. If he is interested in sport, he may be out for the day either at the international motor-racing track, on the South Dakota circuit near the airport, or watching cricket at the City Cricket Club in Bourda. He could also be playing a game of basketball

A sports ground on the edge of Georgetown, the capital of Guyana. The ground overlooks the sea and the sandy beaches

(a very popular sport in Guyana) in one of the Georgetown stadiums.

As the fishing and fish-processing business cannot wait for holidays, Mr Green may have to work for part of the day. Arriving home at midday he would find the house empty. In the kitchen the remnants of the morning's breakfast—fish, rice and fruit—have been cleared away and Mrs Green has left a snack out for him, such as a dish of Foo-Foo (plantains made into cakes—like potato cakes—and dipped into a very hot pepper sauce). In the refrigerator he will find fruit juice—mango, pawpaw or orange—or a jug of the locally produced refreshing drink called mauby, which is made from the bark of a certain tree.

Mrs Green meanwhile made an early visit to the Stabroek Market on Water Street. She has returned by bus with her shopping—bus fares are very cheap in Georgetown. After dropping the shopping at home, Mrs Green has gone to a local coffee morning where she may be discussing the organization of the Cooperative souvenir shop. Not only does she do a part-time job helping out in the store, she also makes a few items of craftwork for sale to tourists and visitors.

Mrs Green's next-door neighbour may also be at the coffee morning. Mrs Singh is of Indian descent, her grandfather came from Madras, in eastern India, many years ago. The family still keep to the Hindu religion and have enjoyed one of their holy events, Phagwah Day. Mrs Singh and her family live very much like the other 150,000 Indians in Georgetown. The men dress in

Inside a Hindu temple in a small town in Guyana. There are over 150,000 Indians (mostly Hindus) living in Georgetown alone

the dhoti (loose trousers), the women wear the sari. Mrs Singh may be skilled at embroidering colourful saris. The Green and Singh families occasionally visit each other for an evening meal and they each serve their own local dishes. Indian people in Guyana have a diet of curries and rice, chapatties and hot, spicy food; they have made rice the most important food in Guyana and their ancestors brought many Indian habits to Guyana during the last century.

The Green family eat traditional Guyanese food which derives from a mixture of African recipes and Caribbean foods. Pepperpot soup is their favourite. It is one of the most interesting dishes

51

A pepper stall in a Guyanese market. Peppers and hot chillies are popular ingredients in many of the local and traditional dishes

of African origin. Pepper-pot is a hot dish that can be kept cooking for several days or several weeks—it has been known for it to be constantly replenished over a period of years! The ingredients of the "pot", as it is called, are chopped bacon, lamb or beef, green peppers, hot chillies, paprika, cassava juice, calaloo (a Caribbean type of spinach), fish, okra, yam, plantain, suet, flour, lime and onions! Leftovers from other meals are often added to the pepper-pot which is made in a large, black cauldron kept over the heat.

Other local dishes include *metmgee,* a mixture of root vegetables (yams, eddoes, cassava and plantain), cooked in coconut-milk juice. In restaurants like the Kwang Chow in Camp

52

Street, Chinese food can be bought; the Rice Bowl on Robb Street offers Indian and local (Creole) dishes including the hot casareep sauce and cassava cakes. On the Avenue of the Republic a local restaurant also sells the Portuguese speciality called garlic pork. Several of the hotels in Georgetown serve Western or American-type food but, to get the real flavour of Guyanese cookery the visitor's best move is to get an invitation to eat with the Green family, or the Singhs.

A New Colony—A New Nation

Following the establishment of Guyana's first settlement, named in Dutch Kijkorveral ("Overlooking All"), in the early years of the seventeenth century, the country became a colony. This fortified island site, manned by Dutch traders, was the forerunner of a series of settlements. The only evidence of these early structures still remaining are the ruins of Kijkorveral, now a tourist attraction.

There are few buildings in Guyana that are more than one hundred years old. Probably the most ancient structures are those which the visitor does not easily notice. They are the waterways, canals and "dykes"—miniature dams constructed to hold water back from land reclaimed from the sea and lowland areas around Georgetown. The dykes and dams were built by Dutch workers very early on during the original settlement of the coastal region. Most Dutch forts were built high above the surrounding, flat river marshes which often lay below sea level. For this reason, when the British established the city of

The Georgetown City Hall, one of Guyana's finest examples of colonial architecture, in Gothic style

Georgetown in 1781, they employed a similar method of keeping their buildings "high and dry". Even today, approaching Georgetown from the sea, only the highest tips of the lighthouse can be seen above the alluvial flats, the wireless station, the market spire, the twin square church towers and the main hotel, the Pegasus.

In the capital many of the very old buildings were destroyed in a large fire in 1945. This was because so many structures had been built of wood — a very hard local wood which withstands the harsh climatic conditions. The oldest building is the 1852 Guyana House, now the residence of the country's president. The second oldest standing structure is on the High Street — the

Tudor-style Law Courts, completed in 1878. Not far away, on the Avenue of the Republic, is the Gothic-style City Hall, built in 1887. Georgetown's most spectacular structure is said to be the tallest wooden building in the world. It is St George's Cathedral, built in 1892, which has a spire 52 metres (143 feet) high.

Being the main seaport, Georgetown represents the centre of commerce in Guyana. The city is located at the mouth of the Demerara River which all shipping must enter before docking. Stabroek Market, with its Gothic-style clock tower, is on Water Street. The market is the hub of the city and the focal point for shopping and trading. People come from all over the country to

St George's Cathedral in Georgetown — the tallest wooden building in the world

The tower of Stabroek Market in the centre of Georgetown. Almost any commodity can be bought from its numerous stalls

this large, iron-built edifice where almost any commodity can be bought. The site possibly goes back to the earliest days of colonial Guyana when all the country's needs were imported and dispersed through the market-place in Georgetown.

In the early pioneer days the only guaranteed way of travelling in Guyana, before road and rail, was by boat up the numerous large rivers. Most of the rivers in Guyana start life as spectacular waterfalls, way up in the highlands of the south. Many rapids and falls—some of spectacular beauty—break up the long, winding waterways. Most famous of these are the Kaieteur Falls. Other significant natural phenomena include weirs and rapids which present hazards for navigation. By the

One of Guyana's many spectacular waterfalls

time the rivers, like the Demerara, the Berbice, Essequibo and
Potaro, have reached the flat, alluvial plain near the coast, they
have become wide, bending stretches of water, often with islands
formed along their course.

Even large seagoing ships can navigate some of Guyana's
rivers. Because of this it was possible for settlements to be
established in the new colony. Most new townships grew up near
one or other of the large rivers, apart from those already located
along Guyana's coast.

Everything that settlers and colonists needed had to be
transported up the rivers to the new villages and townships.
There were three reasons which drove men to endure the

58

hardships of unexplored territory, including disease, hostile Indians, and the rigours of jungle life.

One reason was the challenge and the pure excitement of discovery—the jungles of Guyana are still attracting explorers.

The second reason was that priests wished to convert the newly-discovered races and tribes to their own religions. Evidence of religious communities established in the late nineteenth and early twentieth centuries can be seen at the first Jesuit mission, founded in 1911 by Cary Elwes at St Ignatius, just outside Lethem town. Other missions and trading-posts were established throughout the country's short history. Most were unable to maintain themselves and soon fell into ruin.

The third, and most important, reason for braving the "New World", was personal gain. Even as far back as Sir Walter Raleigh's exploits and his search for El Dorado in the late sixteenth century, the lure of riches had attracted treasure-seekers to Guyana's wild and untamed hinterland. The hills and mountains of the country did not reveal the Cities of Gold which Raleigh sought. Instead, the ancient rocks of Guyana have revealed large quantities of alluvial gold and diamonds. Many independent, small-scale miners search for these precious minerals in the clay and rocks in most inhospitable conditions. They "pan" for gold in the streams and rivers.

Another, very important deposit found in Guyana is bauxite. This valuable mineral looks like red earth, and is used to make aluminium. Large quantities of it have been found in several places in the country. The most prominent locations for opencast bauxite mining are at Mackenzie, Demba, Ituni and Kwakwani. All these sites are on the shores of the Demerara River, except for Kwakwani which lies on the Berbice. Prospectors for riches, priests in search of souls and explorers in search of fame all contributed to the opening up of Guyana's huge forested region.

Once regular trading routes between outlying settlements and the coastal towns had been established along the courses of the large rivers, the country started to become a unified colony. Until the mid-nineteenth century there was no real identity to the country. The Guianas were, until then, just a vast, unexplored region, full of hostile Indians, impenetrable jungle,

Bauxite and alumina being loaded onto a cargo ship

snakes and wild animals. The real colony of Guyana consisted of a scattering of townships along, or just inland, from the coast.

Twenty-two little farmsteads had been carved out of the bush and forest areas in the hills. The farmers tried to grow coffee, cotton, tobacco and sugar but, by the mid-eighteenth century, most had succumbed to famine and disease and been driven back to the easily farmed coastlands. Only thirteen of these early clearings survived after 1880. Similarly, diamond- and gold-prospectors, just a handful of courageous Dutchmen and Englishmen, battled "white-water" rapids and terrible hardships in order to recover precious minerals from riverbeds and cliff-faces. The treacherous terrain claimed many lives but, over the centuries, the colony became established and Guyana acquired its identity—and its borders.

Today, from the air, little has changed in the country's interior. The abandoned attempts at plantation clearing can be seen as patches in a "sea" of green jungle. Only the rivers, which snake through the dense undergrowth, break up the green carpet of trees. Alongside some of the rivers are townships like Kumaka, Linden, Mackenzie and Bartica. Bauxite-mining, started in 1916, shows as big open scars linked by roads and tracks through forest and bush.

Few roads are noticeable until nearer the Atlantic coast. Springlands, on the border with Surinam and on the Courantyne River, is linked through Georgetown to Charity on the Pomeroon River. The coast road is almost 300 kilometres (185 miles) long, and river crossings are made by ferry except for

A memorial to Willian Russell, a British explorer who founded a settlement in a jungle clearing in the 1800s

the route across the Demerara, which is crossed by the recently constructed Demerara harbour bridge. Some roads open up the interior of Guyana, like those to the gold- and diamond-mining fields. Many of the roads are still just trails through the bush but they are important links which unify the nation.

Guyana has the oldest operating railway outside the United Kingdom—although it is less than 100 kilometres (60 miles) in length. Freight is carried by road and by Guyana Airways which operate out of Timehri International Airport near Georgetown. Large quantities of freight are also carried on the rivers and through Guyana's ports of Georgetown, New Amsterdam and Springlands, plus some secondary harbours. Many of the boats seen in Georgetown harbour are ocean-going steamships but the country's fishing fleet, based in the capital's harbour, has about one hundred shrimp trawlers.

If the interior of Guyana is one great carpet of forest and jungle broken by mountain peaks and criss-crossed by rivers, the flat alluvial plain which runs along the coastline is a strip of ricefields and agricultural land interrupted by the wide mouths and estuaries of many large rivers. Guyana is green and brown from the Atlantic coastline, right up to the Brazilian border 600 kilometres (400 miles) into the interior. It is difficult to see where people have "made their mark" on the countryside. This is

A sugar-loading bay in the busy Georgetown harbour

because the tropical climate encourages the foliage to grow thick and fast.

It is these forests and jungles which have prevented people "digging deep" into the countryside. But the trees and bushes themselves are becoming important to the establishment of this new nation. For years the people of Guyana have been using the great timbers from the forests to build their homes, but now the export of these forest "giants" is an important part of the Guyanese economy and helps to support the emergent nation.

Plants, Animals and Tourist Attractions

Food production takes priority in Guyana, and more people are employed in the agricultural sector than in services or industry. Self-sufficiency of the population has been achieved from growing rice, coconuts, bananas, tropical fruit, maize, plantains and vegetables, although the population's main source of protein comes from Guyana's thriving fishing industry.

About thirty per cent of export earnings come from the sale of agricultural produce, including sugar, rum and sugar products. Coffee and cocoa contribute to the export drive and more than fifty per cent of total exports come under the category of food.

Because the country is predominantly wooded, the main region of agricultural activity is on the flat coastal plain. This region produces more than a quarter of the country's wealth. Just five per cent of the country, mainly in the hills and savannah, is used as pastureland for grazing cattle and sheep. Today, meat is transported to the towns and the coast by air instead of on the hoof in herds. Both in the hills and on the coast there are small plots of land which produce household needs such as fruit and vegetables, or larger co-operative plots which are run as market gardens.

Quite substantial quantities of some crops are grown such as mangoes, pineapples, avocados, oil palms, pawpaw, sapodilla, tangerines, oranges and the local speciality known as five-fingers, or carambola. Some of these tropical, exotic fruits are canned for export. Many people grow small crops of root and tuber vegetables such as sweet potatoes, yams, eddoes, cassava and groundnuts (peanuts). Peppers and hot spices figure in most Guyanese meals, especially as many people are of Indian origin and enjoy curries. Therefore, almost every little garden plot has a small patch set aside for spices, herbs and peppers.

An unxpected occupation for people from such an isolated country, although it may be not so unusual because of the

An orange stall in a Guyanese market

A pawpaw tree growing in a garden on the outskirts of Georgetown

tropical climate and lush vegetation, is the work of botanists and flower-growers. A number of Guyanese earn a living from cultivating flowers for sale. Some of the world's most colourful and exotic flowers grow easily in the country's rich soil and in its warm, humid climate.

The giant-leaved Victoria Regis lake lily is famous because its round, flat leaves spreading out across the water are said to be strong enough to support the weight of a five-year-old child! The Victoria Regis is Guyana's national flower and it appears on the country's coat-of-arms. Orchids grow well in the Guyanese forests as do the helicona, the yellow allamanda and a flower called tiger-beard. On the highest mountain, Mount Roraima, there grows an insect-eating flower called the pitcher plant. The marabunta is one of the most popular of local flowers.

Right up high in the jungles and forests grow a large variety of important trees. Most people think of palm trees when they hear the word "tropical". Many types of palm trees do grow in Guyana, of course, but the important ones are those which produce oil (the oil palm), coconuts (the coco palm) and dates (from the rarer, date palm.) There are also decorative palms such as the royal palm, the traveller's palm and the very tall trees which are cut as timber because they are either extremely hard or decorative when cut and polished. The greenheart and the wallaba are among the most commercially sought after trees but the mora, locust, crabwood and purple heart trees are also valuable for their wood.

In the gardens of Guyana the annatto tree can be seen. This has been known since Carib Indian times for its vegetable dye giving an orange tinge to foods like cheeses. The cannonball

Bora (a kind of runner bean) ready for market. Many people in Guyana grow their own food produce and sell the surplus

A cup of gold—one of the many beautiful flowers in a range of brilliant colours to be found in Guyana's tropical forests

tree, so-called because its fruits are the size and shape of rusty cannonballs, can also be seen. This tree and its fruit must be avoided because it contains a deadly poison. Even in the dark forests there are trees and plants which should be avoided; the spiny-toothed leaves of the bromeliads can cut severely and the juice of the tree called strychnos is used by the Indians on blow-pipe darts to poison their prey. This sap is known as "curare".

Above the mountains the rare harpy eagles wheel and swoop. In the jungles a multitude of colourful butterflies and birds can be seen, including cock-of-the-rock, hummingbirds, parrots and toucans. The national bird, the conje pheasant, nests between the roots of giant trees. Frogs and snakes also thrive in these dank, moist conditions. The most famous is probably the giant

69

The short-lived hibiscus blossom, typical of the country's exotic flowering plants and shrubs

anaconda, a snake which can grow to a fearful size and which is at home as much in the water as on land. This reptile is not poisonous, but it can crush its prey to death and has been known to swallow even a fully-grown calf whole!

Sharing the rivers with the anaconda are the notorious piranha fish of South America. Locals call the piranha *perai*. In shoals, this fish can tear a dead sheep to pieces within seconds. By contrast, a harmless, but giant fish, common in the rivers of Guyana and very good to eat, is the huge arapaima. The arapaima can grow to four metres (twelve feet) in length and can

70

weigh up to 135 kilograms (300 pounds). Another fascinating fish found in these waters is the electric eel. Really a catfish, this creature can deliver a shock equivalent to 500 volts! Some other fish have extraordinary names such as the sunfish, hassar, patua and lukunani. The manatee—sea-cow or *manjuari*—inhabits the river estuaries. Sailors of old used to misname these large, seal-like mammals "mermaids".

Down at the edges of the rivers—the best place to see wildlife

A harpy eagle in the jungle

in a jungle—a number of mammals can be seen taking a wary drink. They have to be careful because caimans (similar to alligators) are common in Guyana's many rivers. Among the animals on the river bank it is possible to spot the jaguar, the pride of Guyana. The jaguar is the largest of the South American cats and it appears on the coat-of-arms of the country. Pumas and the smaller ocelot live in the rainforests as do numbers of small deer which often fall prey to the large cats. The capybara, the world's largest rodent, also lives in fear of the pumas and jaguars.

On the forest floor anteaters scavenge for food with

A pair of giant turtles being hauled out of the fishing-net

Caimans—like this one—are common in Guyana's rivers

armadillos and *eira,* or coatis (which are like little racoons). By far the largest animals to be found in Guyana, apart from the big cats, are the curious tapirs, which are related to the horse and the hippopotamus. Wild pigs and the boars called peccaries snout around the roots of giant trees and lianas. Several types of monkeys, like the sakiwinka, leap and scream through the hanging vines high above the forest floor.

Iguanas and lizards are native to Guyana and so are vampire bats. Vampire bats generally avoid humans but will quite often take blood from horses or cattle whilst they are sleeping. The greatest danger from vampire bats is that they can pass on the near-fatal disease called rabies. Another creature with a fearsome reputation is the Guyanese bird-eating spider—the largest arachnid in the world.

Tourism has been a godsend to many countries when the price of sugar came down and there was no market for it in Europe and the United States. Because the climate and scenery on many Caribbean islands is so pleasant to people from temperate zones, visitors like to spend their holidays in the sun and on the beaches. Tourists bring money to spend on hotel accomodation, on travelling in the countries and on buying food and gifts. It was, and still is, this money that saved some of the islands from economic disaster and from having to depend for their survival on loans from larger, richer countries.

In Guyana this transition did not occur because the nature of the country is different from that of a tropical, Caribbean island. The most adventurous travellers, and those who want a more exciting and more active holiday than just sitting on a sandy beach, are beginning to select countries like Guyana for their vacations. Guyana does not offer white beaches and clear blue seas, but it does offer the excitement of roaring waterfalls, giant rivers, jungles and forests, great mountains and a wonderful selection of trees, plants, fruit and flowers, wildlife, birds, fish, butterflies and insects; not to mention the Indians who live deep in the country's interior.

All these attractions are exactly what the more ambitious tourist and visitors wants to see. At the moment, the traveller in

A Guyanese waterfall—a typical tourist attraction

Guyana must undergo a certain amount of discomfort since the country lacks the modern amenities associated with tourism. However, in order to make things easier for visitors and therefore bring tourist money into the country, the government and some enterprising concerns are preparing several sites throughout the country for people brave enough to endure a little less comfort than can be found on a Caribbean beach!

Rum and Rice, Minerals and Timber

Every country in the world depends on trade. Trade balances the economy. If a country produces only oil, electrical goods or sugar, it can exchange its surplus (the items in excess of local demand) for items or goods which they do not make or grow.

Guyana first looks to its natural resources for commodities which can be used in the country or exchanged for goods from other countries. When explorers first looked at the rocks, trees and natural resources, they found that Guyana had some areas rich in gold and diamonds, some areas which were good for fruit-growing and others which had soil conditions ideal for growing crops such as sugar and rice. Later, the explorers found that some rocks contained bauxite. They also recognized that some of the trees which grow in Guyana could be sold for use in other countries. These trees are known as precious woods.

When a country looks at its natural resources the first concern is to feed, clothe and house its people. The Amerindian tribes who originally inhabited Guyana did not demand much. They

Characteristic scenery and homes in the countryside of Guyana. The economy today is based on both agriculture and industry

"lived off the land"—whatever they found in the forests or rivers, they used or adapted in one way or another as shelters, tools, clothes and food.

The people who colonized Guyana—about 350 years ago—wanted better conditions and living standards than the Indians. At first, the settlers had to import everything they needed from their home countries in Europe. Ships brought goods and commodities—plus more people! In return, the ships took back to Europe tropical plants and fruit, precious wood and timber, gold and diamonds. The settlers grew vegetables and introduced pigs, goats and chickens for food. Some colonists grew more than they needed themselves and created a trade in food or produce which they had grown. Some started growing plants which thrived in the tropical climate of Guyana and its special

77

type of soil. Sugar was one of those crops which was introduced into Guyana; so was rice. During the early colonial days sugar and sugar-products became very popular in Europe. All over the Caribbean region, planters began growing the crop in vast sugar-cane fields.

Growing and processing sugar in Guyana became so important that it became the country's main industry. Even today, the growing of sugar and manufacturing of sugar-products is one of the country's major businesses. Much more than just sugar is obtained from the plant. The distilled spirit, rum, is produced from sugar-cane; medical and industrial alcohol is also extracted from sugar; molasses, syrup, treacle and some chemicals are all by-products of cane; and, what is left—the

Freshly bagged sugar outside a factory in Guyana. Sugar is still an important crop in spite of competion from European sugar-beet

bagasse—is also made use of in making paper, cardboard and chipboard, and for fuel.

Between 1838 and 1917, a great number of people from India and Asia flocked to Guyana. These people were not used to the type of food the African slaves had been eating; they were also not familiar with the diet of the European colonists and planters. The Indians and Asians brought their own recipes and foods with them. Rice is the staple food of most of the people who live in Asia and it was rice which the Indians brought with them and which they planted in abundance. By 1917, nearly all the agricultural farming on the coastal strip was sugar-cane fields or "paddy"—ricefields. Almost 200,000 tonnes of rice is now being grown in the country and about four million tonnes of sugar is being produced. Much of the rice is for local consumption; most of the sugar is destined for export. There are now only thirteen sugar plantations currently in production.

Alas, the cultivation of sugar-cane is not now as important as it used to be a century or so ago. European farmers have developed sugar-beet—a kind of root crop which contains sugar and which will grow almost anywhere. Sugar-beet has become an important source of sugar and sugar-products. The many countries, including Guyana, which once earned their income from selling sugar-cane products have found themselves with large surplus quantities of the crop. However, as Guyana is such a large country and as it contains rocks and soil which are rich in minerals, the economy of the country was not so crucially dependent on sugar.

Bauxite-mining in Guyana began after the First World War, in about 1919. Countries like Canada, which already had a great deal of experience in producing aluminium, contributed machinery and technology to help Guyana extract the bauxite from the rocks and earth. To extract alumina (the main ingredient in processing aluminium) from bauxite requires large amounts of energy which is expensive and which must be created on the refining site. However, as Guyana has such vast resources of bauxite, and other countries are willing to pay a great deal for the alumina, Guyana is able to offset the cost of the energy production against the valuable foreign income from the end-product. Therefore, as Guyana is the world's seventh largest producer of bauxite, it is relatively wealthy in this product alone.

Being able to supply foreign countries with large amounts of sugar, sugar products and bauxite, does not constitute a balanced economy. People want food, houses, clothes, cars, televisions, refrigerators and all the items and commodities which go to make up a good, modern standard of living. The foreign money recovered from selling sugar and alumina cannot pay for all the requirements of a population totalling around one million people.

Guyana produces a large proportion of food which its population consumes—rice, fish, roots and tubers (like potatoes), green vegetables, tropical fruit, coconuts, some dairy and beef cattle, pigs, sheep and goats. Some of the agricultural land also produces food for livestock and some is used as pasture. However, more than eighty-five per cent of the entire area of Guyana is covered by forest or jungle.

The hardwoods and precious woods found deep in the interior of Guyana are in great demand from countries which manufacture furniture and decorative items from such timber as wallaba and greenheart. Much of the timber cut from the forests is sold abroad and some is used domestically in the nation's construction programme—building homes, bridges, riverside installations—and also as scaffolding for erecting office blocks and public buildings. In Guyana there is a thriving shipbuilding industry and some boats are constructed from local woods. Guyanese carpenters and cabinet-makers assemble

Newly-built houses in a Guyanese town. Local timber is used for domestic construction and is exported to other countries

furniture and carve household items from some of the valuable woods.

With an important trade in rum, sugar and sugar-products, rice, bauxite and alumina, precious timber, as well as a fishing export industry and the production of some gold and diamonds, Guyana earns enough to pay for the basic needs of its population. The price that Guyana can charge for its sugar and its bauxite has dropped over the past few years and that has meant that the country has had to borrow an increasing amount of money in order to keep an economic balance.

Some people say that because Guyana has so many big, fast-flowing rivers and a constant supply of water, the government could build large hydro-electric dams which would be able to produce electricity and energy for industry, to light homes and offices and run machinery. Scientific explorers also say that there is oil under the ground in Guyana which could supplement the import of costly oil from other countries. The reason that Guyana cannot yet construct major hydro-electric schemes, or drill its own supply of oil, is that both these operations are very expensive. The building of hydro-electric dams and energy-producing schemes from natural sources like rivers and waterfalls, costs a great deal in terms of money and skills. It will, therefore, be some time before these ideas can be put into practice.

With only a limited amount of money to spend on development and with a growng population, the principal

Outside a Georgetown hospital. As in most countries of the world, more funds are needed to improve the healthcare facilities

demands on the country's budget are the services which immediately affect the people. Health—nursing, doctors, hospitals, clinics and medicines; education—teachers, books, schools and equipment; defence—army, patrol-launches, air-craft, and the police force; agricultural development—food production, clothing and housing. All these take their share of the money any country has available. Guyana is no exception. Its people are concerned first and foremost about those issues which affect them directly.

Guyana Today—One Destiny

"One People, One Nation, One Destiny" is the motto on the Guyana coat-of-arms. It signifies the aims of a country which has been formed from many races, from divided territories and with varied aims. Now well-established, Guyana has a long struggle ahead in order to reach all its goals.

Unlike the other twenty-four Caribbean countries which, except French Guiana are all islands, the country of Guyana has no direct reliance on tourism as a source of income. The Caribbean islands and island groups are committed to earning a good percentage of their foreign income from tourists. Guyana is more an agricultural and mining country. Its reliance on produce can be seen in the national emblem or coat-of-arms. The two jaguars on each side of the centre shield are holding a mining pickaxe on the left and a stalk of sugar-cane on the right. In the Indian head-dress above the shield are two diamonds. The pickaxe indicates bauxite mining, the cane stands for the sugar industry and the diamonds for the gemstone-mining.

Just as the national emblem reveals the country's main activities in industry, so Guyana's national anthem refers to the unity of the people and the country's natural beauty. The title of the anthem is *Dear Land of Guyana, of Rivers and Plains*. This echoes the Amerindian name, Guyana: "Land of Many Waters". In the national flag there is also a reference to the land, the people and the political unity of Guyana's mixed races. Red, yellow, black and white stripes make up a large arrow on a green background symbolizing the green countryside and the combination of peoples in the land.

Guyana achieved independence on 26 May, 1966. The national identity was created and the name changed from British Guiana (a colony) to Guyana—an independent, co-operative republic within the Commonwealth, as from 23 February, 1970. The official name for the country is The Co-operative Republic of Guyana. It has had a continuous, democratic administration for more than twenty-five years. Guyana has a parliament and is presided over by a president and a prime minister. The prime minister is the head of the government. A constitution was written on 6 October, 1980. The constitution provides for the rule of law.

To celebrate independence the people of Guyana erected a large aluminium archway in the capital, Georgetown. Several other monuments are to be seen in the city. Most, like the Cuffy monument to the slave rebellion and the Namibia monument, celebrate important events both in Guyana and in countries with which Guyana is sympathetic.

85

A rally of the People's National Congress, Guyana's ruling party

Georgetown is a pretty and elegant capital, with its white-painted wooden buildings contrasting with modern structures like the Satellite Earth Station dish, or the Cultural Centre which is said to house the best theatre in the Caribbean. Sports stadiums and facilities include those for football and cricket, a motor-racing track, badminton and lawn tennis courts, a cycle-track and hockey-field. Guyana's National Sports Development Council is promoting many other sporting activities—the country is world renowned for boxing champions.

There are several new housing developments in progress in Georgetown and its outskirts. These, together with plans for road improvements and transport schemes, show that Guyana is constantly improving its facilities.

As Guyana was once a British colony and dependent on

Britain for government organization and economic development, the country has a close tie with Europe in general. Britain is especially concerned with improving conditions in its former colony and is Guyana's major trading partner. A number of private and public British companies are involved in several important schemes to keep Guyana on the road to unified prosperity.

Guyana is linked with the European Economic Community (EEC). This is an organization of twelve European countries which also help their ex-colonies (called the ACP—African, Caribbean and Pacific states). There are sixty-six ACP states and

A view of old Georgetown

Work in progress on one of Guyana's new construction sites

Guyana comes under the Caribbean section. A great deal of European money is spent assisting these ACP states and many programmes help in health, food, construction, industry, housing, trade and cultural projects. Guyana benefits in several ways from the EEC policy.

The EEC also supports organizations which physically get the necessary work done. Health is a main concern of the EEC assistance in Guyana. Any outbreak of disease (like malaria) must be eradicated immediately in order to preserve the high level of national health. The EEC also supports other programmes, supplies machinery and advises on training Guyanese in operating industrial equipment, in construction and in finance.

The Commonwealth Development Corporation (CDC) is

88

projects, and involvement in timber exploitation in the Guyanese forests. Another helpful organization is the Overseas Develop-ment Institute (ODI) which is designed to help in social and economic development. The United Nations also provides great support to projects which influence Guyana's progress. The Centre for World Development Education (CWDE), advises on projects and development programmes in countries like Guyana and informs on current projects which the World Bank has made possible. (The World Bank is an organization which provides funding for hundreds of projects in developing countries.) Health schemes, transport improvement and irrigation are just a few of the development programmes in Guyana which the World Bank has supported.

New housing on the outskirts of the capital—this is the face of the modern prosperous Guyana being built for the future

tion are just a few of the development programmes in Guyana which the World Bank has supported.

There are also many specialist organizations which provide advice, aid, training, finance and technical skills in Guyana — to medical and health associations, education and training schemes, forestry and mining institutes, agricultural and industrial establishments and other groups which have taken an interest in Guyana's future. By these means the country is progressing cautiously towards a prosperous future.

Index